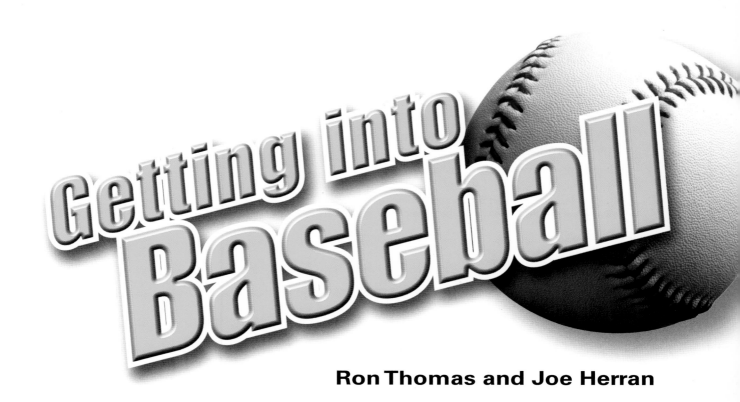

Getting into Baseball

Ron Thomas and Joe Herran

CHELSEA HOUSE
PUBLISHERS
A Haights Cross Communications ® Company ®
Philadelphia

This edition first published in 2006 in the United States of America by Chelsea House Publishers, a subsidiary of Haights Cross Communications.

A Haights Cross Communications ✈ Company ®

Chelsea House Publishers
2080 Cabot Boulevard West, Suite 201
Langhorne, PA 19047-1813

The Chelsea House world wide web address is www.chelseahouse.com

First published in 2005 by
MACMILLAN EDUCATION AUSTRALIA PTY LTD
627 Chapel Street, South Yarra 3141

Visit our website at www.macmillan.com.au

Associated companies and representatives throughout the world.

Copyright © Ron Thomas and Joe Herran 2005

Library of Congress Cataloguing-in-Publication Data Applied for.
ISBN 0 7910 8808 1

Edited by Helena Newton
Text and cover design by Cristina Neri, Canary Graphic Design
Page layout by Karen Young
Illustrations by Nives Porcellato and Andy Craig
Photo research by Legend Images

Printed in China

Acknowledgments
The author and the publisher are grateful to the following for permission to reproduce copyright material:

Front cover: Baseball player courtesy of Getty Images; baseball courtesy of Photodisc.

AAP/AP Photo/Edmonton Sun-Darryl Dyck, p. 29 (top); Otto Greule Jr/Getty Images, p. 27; John Reid III/MLB Photos/Getty Images, p. 26; Photodisc, pp. 1, 6, 7, 24; Picture Media/Reuters, pp. 4, 5, 22, 28, 29 (bottom); Picture Media/Reuters/Sam Mircovich, p. 30; Picture Media/Reuters/ Peter Morgan, p. 23.

While every care has been taken to trace and acknowledge copyright, the publisher tenders their apologies for any accidental infringement where copyright has proved untraceable. Where the attempt has been unsuccessful, the publisher welcomes information that would redress the situation.

J-Nf

Contents

Glossary words

When a word is printed in **bold**, you can look up its meaning in the Glossary on page 31.

The game

Baseball is played by people of all ages in more than 100 countries around the world. It is played by **amateurs** at local and state levels and by **professionals** in national and international competitions, including the Olympic Games.

The biggest professional baseball league is Major League Baseball (MLB), which runs the professional baseball league and sets the rules for baseball in the United States and Canada. The best baseballers from around the world compete in this league. There are also major professional leagues in Japan and Latin America. At international and Olympic levels, the International Baseball Federation (IBAF) organizes the Baseball World Cup, the International Cup, and the Olympic baseball tournament.

The Boston Red Sox and the New York Yankees (pitching) compete in a Major League Baseball game in New York.

The history of baseball

Many people believe that baseball evolved from an English game known as rounders. Rounders was popular in England during the 1600s. In rounders, the batting player hit the ball with a bat and ran around four **bases**. Fielding players threw the ball at the runner to prevent the runner from scoring. Baseball began in the United States, where the first official game was played in the 1840s in New York City. In 1845, the first rules were developed.

Playing a game

The aim of the two teams playing a baseball game is to score more runs than the opposing team. Each team has a total of nine players. Four umpires, one on each base, control the game.

The visiting team bats first. The batting players take turns to try to hit a ball pitched to them by the opposing team's pitcher. When a ball is hit into fair territory, which is the space inside the **diamond**, the batter attempts to run to first base. When a ball is hit into foul territory, which is the space outside the diamond, the batter cannot run. A run is scored when a batter has run around all of the bases and crossed **home plate** safely. The players on the opposing team in the field try to get the batting team out by catching a hit ball "on the fly" or by **tagging** a runner. The batting team's **inning** is over when three players are out.

Members of the batting team who are not batting or running sit in the dugout during an inning.

A baseball game is played over nine innings. If the game is tied after nine innings, extra innings are played. To win, one team needs to score more runs than the other after each team has had an equal number of extra innings. A Major League Baseball game lasts between one and a half and four hours, depending on the number of runs scored.

Equipment

Equipment such as balls, bats, gloves, and bases used in competition must meet the standards set by Major League Baseball or by local leagues.

Baseball

A baseball is round and made of white real or artificial leather, stitched with heavy red thread. It measures between 9 and 9.25 inches (22.9 and 23.5 centimeters) around and weighs between 5 and 5.25 ounces (141.7 and 148.8 grams). Inside the ball, a small cork center is surrounded by layers of rubber and yarn.

A bat and ball

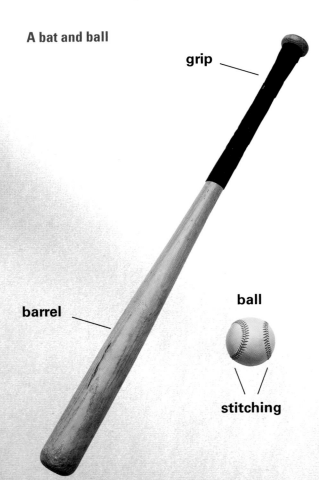

grip

barrel

ball

stitching

Bats

Bats are made of either smooth pieces of wood, usually ash, or of aluminum. A bat must be no longer than 42 inches (107 centimeters) and no wider than 2.63 inches (6.7 centimeters) at its widest point. The handle is covered with a rubber or leather grip and has a knob on the end. The part of the bat that hits the ball is known as the barrel.

Did you know?

Aluminum bats are used by most amateur players because they last longer, but wooden bats must be used in professional baseball.

Clothing

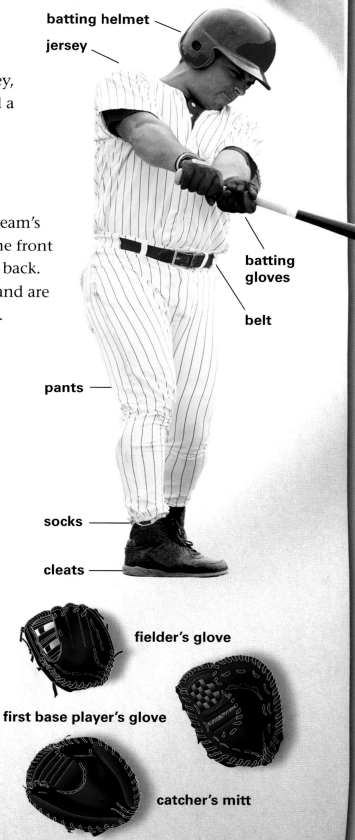

batting helmet

jersey

batting gloves

belt

pants

socks

cleats

Male and female baseballers wear a jersey, pants, shoes known as cleats, socks, and a cap to protect them from the sun.

Jersey, pants, and belt

The loose-fitting baseball jersey has a button-up front and short sleeves. The team's logo or name is usually written across the front and the player's number appears on the back. Pants are made of lightweight material and are worn with a buckled, stretch elastic belt.

Shoes and socks

Shoes are lightweight and made of synthetic leather. Metal cleats in the soles improve a player's balance and speed on grass. Often the shoes are called cleats. Socks have a fitted heel and toe and a cushioned half-sole for comfort.

Protective clothing

Batters wear protective helmets, often with a chinstrap and face mask. Leather batting gloves must fit well to protect the hands and help the batter grip the bat. The catcher wears a protective plastic cap, a mask, a chest protector, knee pads, and shin guards. Fielding players also wear a protective glove.

fielder's glove

first base player's glove

catcher's mitt

Different gloves worn by fielding players

The playing field

Baseball fields are called diamonds because from behind home plate the baseball field looks diamond-shaped. The infield is a dirt square with a base at each corner. The outfield is a grassy area, with padded fences to protect running outfielders. Foul lines, running from home plate to the outfield, separate fair territory and foul territory.

Rule

First, second, and third bases must be marked by white canvas bags, which are securely attached to the ground.

The pitcher throws the ball from the pitching mound. There is a white **pitcher's rubber** in the center of the mound. Home plate is a five-sided piece of white rubber. On both sides of home plate there is a box marked to show the batters where to stand while batting. The bases are white, square, canvas bags filled with sand. The catcher stands in a white square called the catcher's box during play.

A baseball diamond

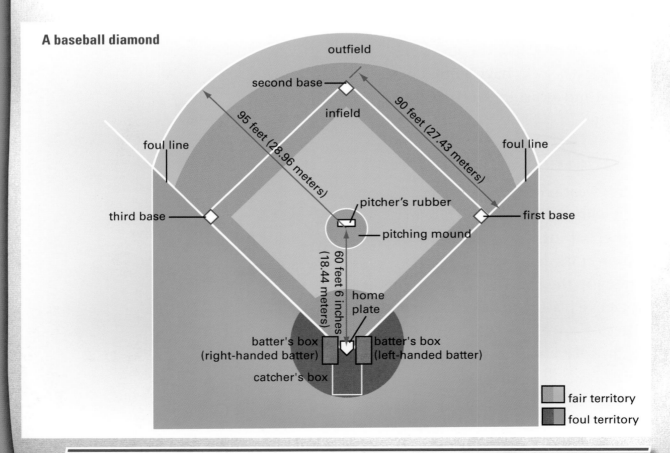

outfield

second base

infield

95 feet (28.96 meters)

90 feet (27.43 meters)

foul line

foul line

third base

pitcher's rubber

pitching mound

first base

60 feet 6 inches (18.44 meters)

home plate

batter's box (right-handed batter)

batter's box (left-handed batter)

catcher's box

fair territory

foul territory

The players

There are nine fielding positions and each player is responsible for a different area of the field. The **battery** consists of the pitcher and the catcher. The pitcher throws the ball across home plate, using difficult pitches to try to force the batter to swing at the ball and miss. This is a **strike**. When a batter misses three pitches, it is a **strike out**. The catcher uses hand signals to tell the pitcher which kind of pitch to throw. The infielders are positioned at first, second, and third base, and shortstop, between second and third base. The infielders try to stop the ball from reaching the outfield. The players in the outfield are the left fielder, center fielder, and right fielder. The outfielders run and catch the ball if it reaches the outfield.

Did you know?

Base coaches stand near first and third base and instruct the runners when to run and when to stay.

The positions of the fielding players, base coaches, and batter

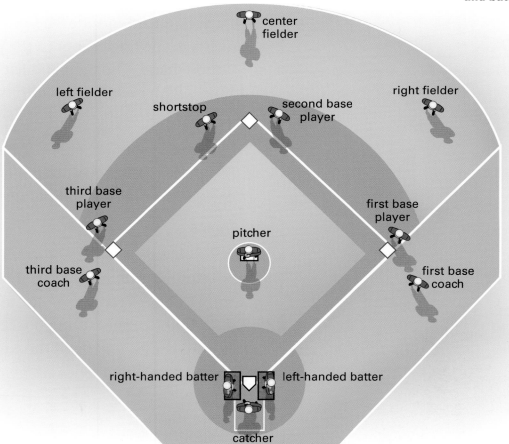

center fielder

left fielder

shortstop

second base player

right fielder

third base player

first base player

pitcher

third base coach

first base coach

right-handed batter

left-handed batter

catcher

Skills

The basic offensive skills of baseball are hitting the ball and running between bases. The basic defensive skills are fielding and throwing the ball. Pitchers and catchers need special skills. Pitchers throw the ball to the batter. The catcher crouches behind the batter and catches any balls that are not hit. With practice, players will develop these skills and improve their performance.

The correct batting grip

Batting

To bat well, the player must have a good grip on the bat and a comfortable stance.

Grip

The batter grips the bat so that the tips of the fingers meet the palm of the hand around the bat. The bat rests in the fingers, not in the palm of the hand. The right and left hands touch, with no space between them.

The bat is held at a 45-degree angle behind the right shoulder, or the left shoulder for a left-handed batter. The back elbow is flexed and points down.

Stance

In the correct stance, the batter's feet are apart, slightly wider than shoulder width. The back foot is parallel to the back line of the batting box. The knees are bent slightly and the weight is evenly distributed. The toes point to home plate.

The correct batting stance

Selecting the right pitch

The batter does not have to swing at every pitch. If a pitch is outside the **strike zone**, the batter does not swing and the ball is caught by the catcher. The strike zone is above home plate between the batter's knees and armpits.

Taking a swing

To take a swing, the batter brings the bat forward and shifts his or her weight from the back to the front foot. The batter twists the hips and shoulders to face the pitcher and swings the bat over the plate, trying to hit the ball. The batter continues swinging the bat to the opposite shoulder.

Rule

All players need to wear a protective helmet while batting.

Taking a swing at the ball

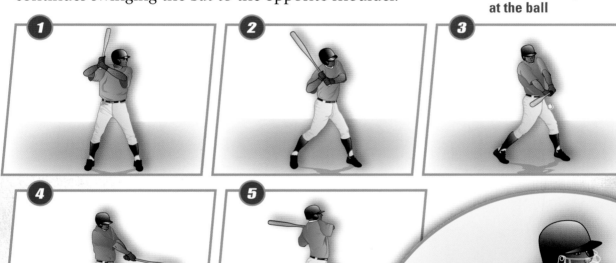

Bunting

Bunting is tapping the ball instead of hitting it. Bunting forces the infielders to run toward the ball and gives the batter more time to get to first base. To bunt the ball, the batter faces the pitcher, holding the bat at chest height with one hand halfway up the bat. The bat is held away from the body and parallel to the ground. The batter taps the ball toward the baseline.

Bunting the ball

Running the bases

After hitting the ball, the batter runs as fast as possible to first base. The batter needs to make contact with the base, using any part of the body, before the fielder on first base tags the batter or reaches the base before the batter while holding the ball. The batter watches the first base coach, who will signal whether or not the batter should stop at first base or keep running to second base.

The leadoff

The leadoff occurs when a runner on a base takes a few steps toward the next base when the pitcher begins the next pitch. This gives the runner a head start toward the next base when the ball is hit. However, if the runner is caught off the base and is tagged by a fielder, the runner is out.

Sliding

To slide into base, the player drops gently to the ground by first bending both knees and then extending one leg toward the base. The back leg is tucked under the runner's body with the toe pointing backward. The player leans back, keeping the head and shoulders upright and facing forward.

Rule

Players are not allowed to run beyond 3 feet (1 meter) on either side of the baseline when running the bases.

Sliding makes it difficult for a fielder to tag a runner because the extended foot is a small target.

Stealing

At any time during play, a base runner can decide to run to the next base. If the player reaches the next base without being tagged, this is known as stealing a base. Before stealing the base, the player tries to get a good leadoff of at least three steps. The base runner watches the pitcher closely in case he or she suddenly throws the ball to a fielder to try to tag the runner out.

A runner stealing a base

Tagging up

A base runner may run to the next base when a **fly ball** is hit. A fly ball is a ball that is hit high into the air. Once the ball is caught, the runner must touch the base he or she is leaving before running to the next base. This is called tagging up. The runner is safe if he or she gets to the next base before being tagged with the ball by an infielder.

Did you know?

On reaching first base, a player can touch and run past the base without being tagged out. But once the runner turns and runs toward second base, he or she can be tagged out by a fielder.

Pitching

The main job of the pitcher is to throw the ball to the batter, keeping it in the strike zone. The pitcher throws the ball in a way that makes it difficult for the batter to hit. The pitcher wears a glove on the non-throwing hand.

To begin, the pitcher stands with both feet facing the batter, with the ball hidden from the batter inside the glove.

The pitcher takes a step back to make contact with the rubber and raises the hands just above the forehead.

Turning sideways and lifting the glove-side knee across the front of the body, the pitcher balances on one foot.

The pitcher takes the throwing arm straight back.

As the pitcher steps forward and turns to face the batter, the throwing arm comes up and over. The ball is released as the foot hits the ground.

After releasing the ball the pitcher faces home plate and is ready to field.

Types of pitches

Pitchers throw different types of pitches to confuse the batter and make it difficult for him or her to hit the ball. The way the pitcher grips the ball determines which pitch is thrown.

Fastball

A fastball is a pitch thrown at full speed directly toward home plate. A major league pitcher can throw a fastball at 97 to 98 miles per hour (156 to 158 kilometers per hour). The pitch gets to the plate in about 0.42 seconds. A four-seam fastball moves less than a two-seam fastball as it spins and travels a little faster.

Curveball

A curveball is gripped with the index and middle finger on the top of the ball. At the moment of delivery, the pitcher twists the wrist so that the ball heads toward the batter but curves away over the plate.

Changeup

The changeup starts high and looks like a fastball but it travels more slowly and suddenly drops under the bat.

Knuckleball

The knuckleball is a slow pitch that travels at only 60 to 65 miles per hour (97 to 105 kilometers per hour). The pitcher grips the ball with the tips of two fingers and, instead of snapping the wrist, pushes the ball toward the batter.

Four-seam fastball grip

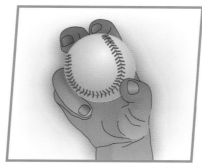

Two-seam fastball grip

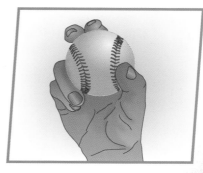

Curveball grip

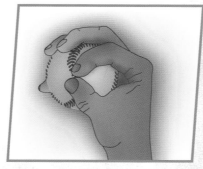

Changeup grip

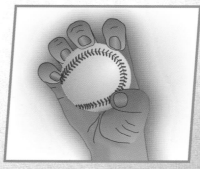

Knuckleball grip

Fielding

Fielders must be fit and able to run fast to catch and then throw the ball. Fielders get the batter out by catching a hit ball before it touches the ground, by tagging a runner, or by tagging a base. There are two types of fielders: infielders and outfielders.

Infielders

Infielders stand at first, second, and third base, and shortstop. Infielders must be alert and ready to move quickly toward a ball that is hit onto the ground.

Before each pitch, the infielders stand in the "ready" position. In this position:

The ready position for a fielder

- the fielder's feet are apart, slightly wider than the shoulders
- the knees are bent and the fielder leans forward with the weight evenly distributed over the balls of the feet
- the hands are between or on the knees.

Fielding a ground ball

To field a **ground ball**, the fielder moves to face the oncoming ball. If the ball is moving slowly, the fielder charges toward the ball. The fielder keeps the glove forward and close to the ground. The throwing hand is above the glove. The fielder looks up and follows the path of the ball. The fielder catches the ball with the glove, then takes the ball out with the throwing hand, straightens up, and throws it to the appropriate base.

Fielding a ground ball

Outfielders

Outfielders need to be able to run fast, catch fly balls, and be able to throw the ball accurately over long distances. The center fielder needs to be the fastest outfielder because he or she has the greatest distances to cover. The right fielder needs strong arms because the throw from right field to third base is the longest throw an outfielder can make. The left fielder needs to be the most reliable fielder since most balls hit to the outfield are hit to left field.

Outfielders must stay alert because much of the game is played in the infield. It is easy for outfielders to become distracted and lose track of what is happening in the game.

Speed

Speed is important because each of the three outfielders has a lot of ground to cover. A fast player can get to a fly ball and catch it to get a member of the opposing team out. Fast outfielders can also get to a ball hit along the ground and return it to the infield to limit the number of bases made by the runners.

Throwing the ball

The fielder holds the ball midway between the fingers and palm and stands side-on to the direction the ball is to be thrown. The fielder takes a short step with the front foot and transfers the weight to the back foot. The throwing elbow is above the shoulder. With the weight on the front foot, the throwing arm is straightened, and the body arches forward as the ball is thrown. After releasing the ball, the arm comes down and follows through.

When throwing, the fielder keeps the eyes on the target.

Outfielders have to throw the ball over longer distances than other fielders. A strong throwing arm that sends the ball to its target quickly can stop a runner from taking bases. If the outfielder does not throw accurately, this can result in an overthrow, which means that the ball misses its target and goes past the fielder to whom it is being thrown. An overthrow usually means that the base runner will be able to take an extra base.

The ready position

Before each pitch the outfielders stand in the "ready" position.
In this position:

- the fielder's feet are apart, slightly wider than the shoulders
- the knees are bent and the fielder leans forward with the weight evenly distributed over the balls of the feet.

Catching the ball

Outfielders need to be able to judge the flight of a fly ball hit into the outfield and run to the spot where they think the ball is going to come down. If the outfielder is unsure where the ball is heading, he or she usually steps back first to track the ball and then runs to where the ball is falling. When running to catch a ball, the outfielder runs on the balls of the feet, keeps the head up, and watches the ball. The outfielder uses both hands to catch the ball.

An outfielder catching a ball

The catcher

The main job of the catcher is to catch pitches that are not hit by the batter. The catcher is also the leader of the team, who positions the fielders and reminds the team of the number of opposing players they have put out in an inning.

Did you know?

During a major league game, up to 60 balls may be used. Until the 1920s, spectators were expected to throw back any balls that were hit into the crowd or out of the field. At major league games today, fans can keep them.

Catcher's stance

Before every pitch, the catcher squats about an arm's length behind the batter with the weight on the balls of the feet. The gloved hand is in the strike zone, giving the pitcher a clear target. The catcher's throwing hand is behind the back to protect it from the pitched ball.

A catcher in the correct stance

Hand signals

The catcher helps the pitcher decide which pitch to throw and where to pitch it, using hand signals. The signals are made with the fingers of the throwing hand, held between the legs. The catcher uses the gloved hand to block these signals from the view of base coaches.

Signaling a curveball

Signaling a fastball

Pop-ups and wild throws

Catchers also need to catch pop-ups, which are balls hit high in the air, usually into foul territory. When a pop-up is hit, the catcher takes the mask off as he or she runs to catch the ball.

When a pitch is "wild"—that is, outside the strike zone—it is the catcher's job to block the ball and quickly return it to the pitcher.

A catcher stopping a wild throw

Rules

Major League Baseball runs the professional baseball league in the United States and Canada. It sets the rules used in most baseball competitions. Players need to learn and understand the basic rules before they are ready to play baseball.

An umpire calling a player out

Some of the rules of baseball are:

- the batter moves to first base if the pitcher throws four balls outside the strike zone (this is called "walking")
- the visiting team bats first
- once three batters are out, the batting and fielding teams change places.

The rules of baseball state that there are five ways a batter can be out. They are:

- strike out, when the batter misses three pitches
- fly out, when the batter hits the ball into the air and the ball is caught in flight
- force out, when the batter or a base runner reaches a base after it has been touched by a fielder who is holding the ball
- tag out, when a batter or base runner is off his or her base and is touched by a fielder who has the ball
- run out, when the base runner leaves the base path while running the bases.

Scoring

There are nine innings in a game of baseball. At the end of nine innings, the team with the most runs wins the game. Runs can only be scored by the batting team. A run is scored when a player touches home plate after he or she has run around the diamond and touched all of the bases in order. A run scored by a player who is able to run and touch all four bases without stopping after hitting the ball is called a **home run**.

Official scorer

The official scorer sits in the stands and keeps the official scorecard. The scorer also makes judgments on whether balls struck are recorded as hits or errors made by the fielding team. The official scorer keeps records of the type of hits batters get, and the way the pitcher and fielders get batters out.

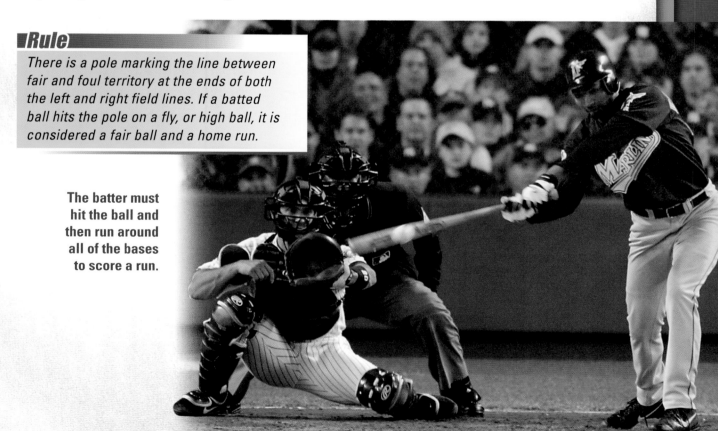

Rule

There is a pole marking the line between fair and foul territory at the ends of both the left and right field lines. If a batted ball hits the pole on a fly, or high ball, it is considered a fair ball and a home run.

The batter must hit the ball and then run around all of the bases to score a run.

Umpires

There are usually four umpires at any baseball game. The most important umpire is the umpire behind the home plate who calls the balls and strikes thrown by the pitcher. The home plate umpire also calls, "Play ball," to signal that the game can begin.

The other umpires are positioned at first, second, and third bases. Their job is to determine whether a runner is out or safe at each base. The umpires on first and third bases also decide whether a ball is fair or foul.

Home plate umpire's gear

The home plate umpire wears special protective gear, including a padded vest, which is usually worn under the uniform, a mask, and leg guards. The umpire's kit bag, attached to the uniform, contains the umpire's indicator, which is a counter to keep track of the balls, strikes, and outs, a plastic plate brush used to brush dirt off home plate, and extra balls to replace any dirty or damaged balls.

The home plate umpire wears protective gear and carries a kit bag.

Umpires' signals

Umpires use hand and arm signals to let players and the scorer know about their decisions, according to the rules of the game.

These are some of the signals used by baseball umpires. The umpire wearing a face mask is the home plate umpire. The umpires without face masks are base umpires.

A stop sign signals "time," meaning that the game has stopped.

Holding up fingers on both hands shows the batter's balls and strikes; two fingers on the right hand and one on the left means two balls and one strike to the batter.

Holding up a number of fingers on each hand indicates how many outs in the inning; one finger on each hand signals "one out."

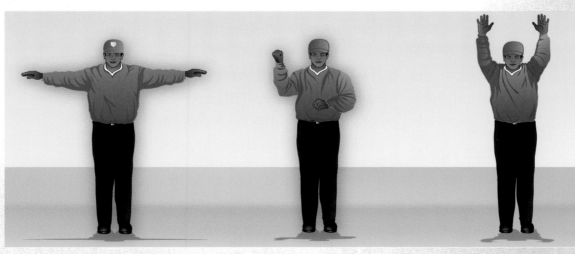

Two arms extended to the sides signals that a batter is safe on a base.

One fist raised signals that the batter is out.

Two arms raised signals a dead ball, meaning a ball has been hit and is not fair or playable.

Player fitness

Baseball players need to be fit if they are to perform to the best of their ability. Running, swimming, and cycling build stamina and fitness.

Warming up and stretching

Before a game or a practice session, it is important for baseball players to warm up all their muscles. This helps prevent injuries such as muscle tears, strains, and joint injuries. Gentle jogging helps players warm up the body. Stretching makes players more flexible and helps the muscles and joints move easily.

The pitcher prepares for the game by throwing a number of pitches to warm up the pitching arm.

Warming up before playing baseball helps prevent injuries.

Neck stretch

The player tilts the head forward then slowly rolls the head to one shoulder and then the other. This exercise will help prevent stiffness in the neck and keep the neck flexible.

Side stretch

The player raises the right hand above the head and slowly leans to the left. The player then repeats the stretch, raising the left hand above the head and leaning slowly to the right. Side stretches are good exercises for pitchers because they need to twist and bend from the waist.

Calf stretch

Placing one foot in front of the other, the player leans forward, but keeps the back heel on the ground. The player pushes forward until he or she feels the calf muscle stretching in the back leg. The stretch is then repeated for the other leg.

Thigh stretch

The player stands on one leg and holds the ankle of the raised leg. The player then pulls the foot back to stretch the thigh. Players can lean against a wall or hold onto another player for balance. The stretch is then repeated for the other leg.

Back stretch

The player crouches down on all fours with the head up and the back flat. Then the player tucks the head in and arches the back. The player feels the stretch in the upper back.

Groin stretch

The player sits on the ground with the knees bent and pointing out to either side. Holding onto the ankles, the player pulls them gently in toward the body. The player pushes down gently on the thighs with the arms so that the legs move toward the ground.

Stretching exercises should be done in an easy and relaxed way and each position should be held for at least 10 seconds.

Competition

People play and enjoy baseball at many levels, both amateur and professional. Baseball leagues run competitions for people of all ages.

Major League Baseball

The largest professional baseball league is Major League Baseball (MLB). Top players from around the world come to North America to play in the 30 teams that represent cities throughout the United States and Canada. These 30 teams form the National League and the American League.

The Major League Baseball season begins in April each year and finishes at the end of September. Each team plays 162 games during the season.

The St. Louis Cardinals celebrate winning a game that allows them to advance to the World Series competition.

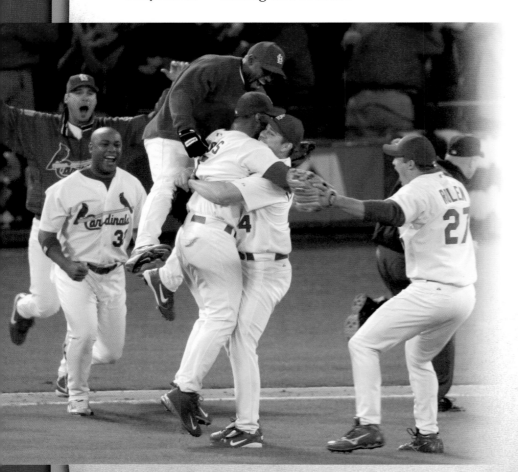

World Series Baseball

At the end of the Major League Baseball season, the top four teams from both the National and American leagues play off for the right to play in the World Series. The World Series is a seven-game competition between the top two teams. The players on the team that wins four games are the world champions.

Women's baseball

There are baseball leagues for women and girls around the world. The countries with the largest leagues are the United States, Canada, Japan, and Australia. In 2001, the first ever World Series was played by these four countries. The World Series is now played each year.

Keri Leamasters of the United States during the 2004 women's baseball World Series

Little League Baseball

In 1939, Carl Stotz formed the first baseball league for boys in Williamsport, Pennsylvania, and named it the Little League. Carl Stotz wanted children to learn sportsmanship, fair play, and teamwork.

Today, Little League Baseball is the world's largest organized youth sports program, with nearly 200,000 teams in the United States and in more than 100 other countries. The Little League Baseball World Series is played every year in Williamsport, Pennsylvania. Players on Little League teams from around the world compete to become the Little League world champions.

Harlem, New York, competed against Worcester, Massachusetts (batting), in the 2002 Little League World Series.

Olympic baseball

Baseball was an Olympic demonstration sport nine times, beginning in 1904. It became an official Olympic sport for men in 1992 in Barcelona, Spain. In Olympic competition, eight teams compete in two four-team divisions. The host country's team, the top four teams from North and South America, the two top teams from Asia, and the top team from Europe compete.

Did you know?

In baseball competitions, the home team usually wears a white or light-colored uniform, while the visiting team wears a darker-colored uniform.

In 1992 and 1996, Cuba won the gold medal. At the 2000 Sydney games, the United States won the gold. In 2000, the International Olympic Committee (IOC) decided that professional baseball players would be allowed to participate in the Olympics for the first time. At the 2004 Athens Olympics, Cuba won the gold medal.

United States baseball player Doug Mientkiewicz heads for home plate, allowing the team to advance to the gold medal round at the 2000 Olympics in Sydney.

Glossary

amateurs	players who do not compete for money
base coaches	coaches who stand near first and third base and tell the runners when to run and when to stay
bases	four corners of a baseball diamond that must be touched by a runner to score a run
battery	the pitcher and the catcher
diamond	the baseball field
fly ball	a ball that is hit into the air
ground ball	a ball that rolls or bounces along the ground after it is hit
home plate	a five-sided piece of white rubber beside which the batter stands and to which the batter must return after running around all of the bases to score a run
home run	when a batter hits the ball and is able to run and touch all four bases without stopping or being tagged out
inning	the period during which both teams get to bat once and play the field once
pitcher's rubber	a narrow platform from which the pitcher pushes off as the ball is thrown to home plate
professionals	players who compete for money
strike	a swing taken at the pitch by the batter that misses, or a ball thrown into the strike zone that the batter does not attempt to hit
strike out	to make three strikes and get out
strike zone	area over home plate between the batter's armpits and the top of the knees
tagging	when a fielder touches a base runner with the ball to put the base runner out

Index